T0099622

SO THAT'S HOW I BEGAN!

SO THAT'S HOW I BEGAN!

THE FACTS ABOUT WHERE BABIES COME FROM

GINA DAWSON

ILLUSTRATED BY ALEX MANKIEWICZ

NEW HOLLAND

CONTENTS

GET THE FACTS

So...
Do you want to know where you came from? That's probably why you have this book, and it's natural to be curious about how babies begin. Some things in this book might seem amazing, weird, embarrassing, or even unbelievable - but everything in this book is true!

Have you heard any stories about where babies come from? There are stories about babies being found under cabbages, amongst the roses or in gooseberry bushes. Or being carried to parents by a large bird called a stork! There are others too... babies found on doorsteps, ordered from hospitals, bought from the shop or delivered by the doctor or mailman.

These stories are told because grown-ups sometimes find it difficult to explain how babies are made, or maybe they think that children are too young to understand.

But you're getting too smart for make-believe stories. You want the facts about families, bodies and how babies are made! It's a fact that...

BABIES BEGIN WITH AN EGG

Not like a chicken's egg... or an ostrich's egg... Of course not! Human babies begin with human eggs!

Human eggs are tiny, soft and round, and don't have crunchy shells. They are kept inside the woman's body. So, to make a baby we need an egg...

AND A SPERM

Sperm are kept inside the man's body. They are very tiny, have wiggly tails and can swim like tadpoles. They need to be fast swimmers because one day they might race to an egg!

But before we get to how that happens, let's have a chat about...

10 9.5

FAMILIES

Families come in lots of shapes and sizes. A family may be two people, or it may be quite a crowd!

A family may have one child, two children or lots of children. It may have two parents, one parent or more. Some children have parents who live in different houses, and they might live with one of parent all the time, or live part of the time with each of them.

Some children have sisters, brothers, step-parents, or step, half or adopted brothers or sisters. Some children have more than one mother or father, and there's lots of ways that can happen. A family may include grand parents, aunts, uncles, and cousins. Some people count their pets as members of their family too!

Two adults who are a couple may create a brand new family by having a baby. That's the way most of us become part of our family - by being born into it.

Another way a child may become part of a family is by being adopted. That's when adults become the parents of a child who needs a family.

Some children are fostered and become part of a foster-family. They might have foster-parents, foster-brothers and foster-sisters, and may stay in contact with their other family as well.

Every family is different and that's okay. But whichever way you became part of your family, you had to be born first! We need a male and a female to make a baby and that's why boys' and girls'...

BODIES ARE DIFFERENT

You've probably noticed that the bodies of boys and girls, men and women, are different. There's a reason for that and it's to do with making babies. Although males and females have most body parts the same, their baby-making parts, or reproductive parts, are different.

Everyone has reproductive parts, and these parts are private regardless of whether a person is a male or female, a child or adult. It's kind of weird that some reproductive parts have "nick-names" and the name you may give them may be different to what someone else calls them, depending on where in the world you live! So I've used the medical terms, that way we don't offend people or get mixed up.

Anyway, a person needs to have an an adult body to make a baby — and that's a VERY good thing because it takes lots of time and work to look after a baby!

So let's take a look at bodies.

THE FEMALE BODY

Women and girls come in all shapes and sizes, wide or narrow, curvy or straight, slender or plump, tall or short. Young girls have flat chests. Women have breasts and that's so if the woman has a baby, her breasts may make milk for the baby to drink.

Women's hips are usually curvier and rounder than girl's hips, and that's so there's more space for a baby to grow inside her body.

FEMALE BABY MAKING PARTS

Inside the female are two ovaries, which are like houses that keep the eggs safe. If an egg leaves an ovary, it can travel through a tube to the uterus, which is also known as the womb. This is the place where a baby grows. The womb is very stretchy, so it starts off small and can make space as a baby grows bigger. Attached to the womb is the vagina, which is the passageway through which the baby is usually born. The vagina goes through to the outside of the body, to the folds of skin that are between female's legs. That's called a vulva, although you may know it as another name.

So they are the parts a woman needs to make a baby.

THE MALE BODY

Men and boys' bodies are all shapes and sizes too, tall or short, muscular or slight, lanky or heavyset, chubby or wiry. Men have narrower hips and wider chests and shoulders, and that is why they are usually stronger than women and children. Some men have hair on their chests too.

MALE BABY MAKING PARTS

On the outside of the male is a bag of skin called a scrotum, and inside that are two testicles. Their job is to make sperm and keep it safe. The sperm can leave the testicles by swimming along some narrow tubes inside the body until they reach the penis. The penis is the tube that's on the outside of the male body. urine, or wee, comes out of the penis, and so can sperm. Only a body that is mature, like a man's body, can make sperm.

So they are the parts that a man needs to make a baby!

COUPLES

The word "couple" means two people who are together, and in this book it means two adults who love and care about each other.

Couples often want to spend as much time together as they can, so they may live together and might choose to get married. Couples have probably met each other's families and many of their friends as well.

Couples may do lots of things together. They may share hobbies or enjoy going out together to fun places. They may help each other with household chores. They will probably enjoy talking with each other and sharing their ideas, plans, opinions and feelings, especially if they are happy, sad, worried or excited. Sometimes they might enjoy holding hands, kissing or cuddling, as it can feel nice to cuddle someone that you love and trust.

MAKING A BABY

Now, I'm going to tell you about a very special cuddle that is just for adults. One name for this special adult cuddle is sexual intercourse. There are other names too, such as sex, or making love.

The couple will choose a comfortable place that is private. Often they'll hop into bed. They might kiss and cuddle, get warm and snuggly, and feel some very special adult feelings. It's difficult to explain these feelings, but they feel nice, and they make the couple want to get closer...and closer... and really, really close to each other.

Sometimes a couple may cuddle so closely that the penis and the vagina fit together! Now that might sound impossible, or awkward or really weird to you, but trust me, for adults who love and care about each other, it is absolutely natural. The couple might wriggle around, kissing and cuddling, because it feels good to be so close.

After a while sperm may leave the man's testicles, swim along the tubes, whiz through the penis and shoot out the end, right into the woman's vagina! And that's when the race to the egg begins!

Having sex is a way that an adult couple can share their love and feelings for each other. Because it can feel very nice and special, the couple may have sex at other times too, not just when they're trying to make a baby!

After the couple has had sex there may be millions of sperm swimming, as fast as they can, in the woman's vagina. Maybe, just maybe, a sperm may win the race and meet an egg. If it does, it will wriggle and burrow its way through the soft egg and that could be the start of a brand new baby!

When the egg and sperm meet we say the egg is fertilized, and after that it usually takes around nine months for the baby to grow inside the mother and be ready to be born.

Now this might be a really good place to stop for a break, and to ask your adult if this was the way that you began.

Most likely the answer will be yes as most babies do begin this way, so then you can skip the whole next page if you want to and start again on the page after.

But if the answer is no and you didn't begin in the way that's just been described, then turn over and keep reading to find out how and why you began in a different way.

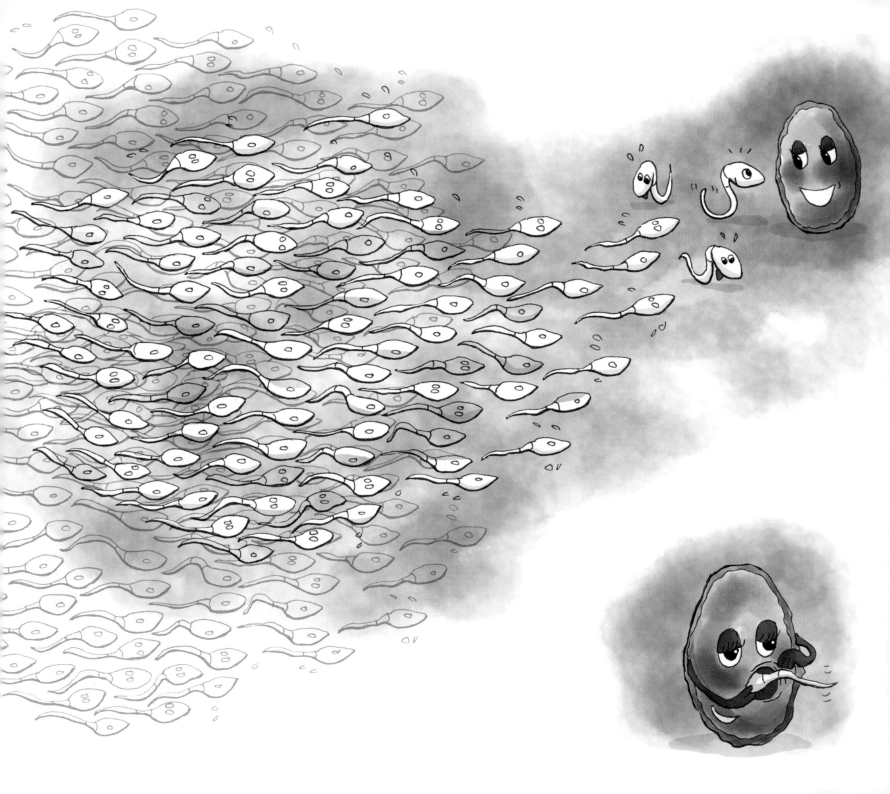

NOT ALL BABIES BEGIN THAT WAY!

Sometimes a couple may want to make a baby but the egg and sperm don't meet. There are many reasons for that. The couple may see a special doctor to find out why, and sometimes the doctor can fix the problem, but that isn't always possible.

The doctor may explain another way to start a baby, called IVF. IVF is when some eggs and sperm are put in a special glass dish, so they don't have far to go to meet each other. If some eggs and sperm meet in the dish, the doctor can pop those fertilized eggs into the woman's womb, where they may continue to grow into a baby.

Not every couple has both healthy eggs and sperm, or may not have either eggs or sperm at all so they will never make a baby through sex or IVF. There's lot of reasons for that, and if the couple want a baby very much, they may choose to use donor eggs or sperm. That's when a kind man with healthy sperm or a kind woman with healthy eggs chooses to give them to the couple, so that they may make a baby. The donor eggs or sperm can then meet with the couple's egg or sperm and that can be the start of a baby too.

So, there's actually several ways to start a baby... most babies begin when an egg and sperm meet through sex! Some begin through IVF, and occasionally babies start with a donor egg or sperm.

IT'S AMAZING!

The start of a new baby is an amazing thing, and it really doesn't matter how each of us began, because it's all okay. And how we began and became part of our family is personal, which means it's usually better not to talk about it with other people until we've discussed it with our family first. Now, once the baby begins inside the mother, it needs to grow, so let's talk about...

THE GROWING BABY "BUMP"

We say a woman is pregnant or expecting once the fertilized egg has attached itself to the inside of her womb. A couple can be very excited when they find out they are expecting a baby!

Some parents are keen to know if their baby is a girl or a boy, so they have a test done by a doctor to find out. Other parents wait until the baby is born and have a surprise.

You may wonder how an egg and sperm somehow turns into a baby, so let's see what happens next. Let's call our growing baby "Bump", because people often call the mother's pregnant tummy a baby bump.

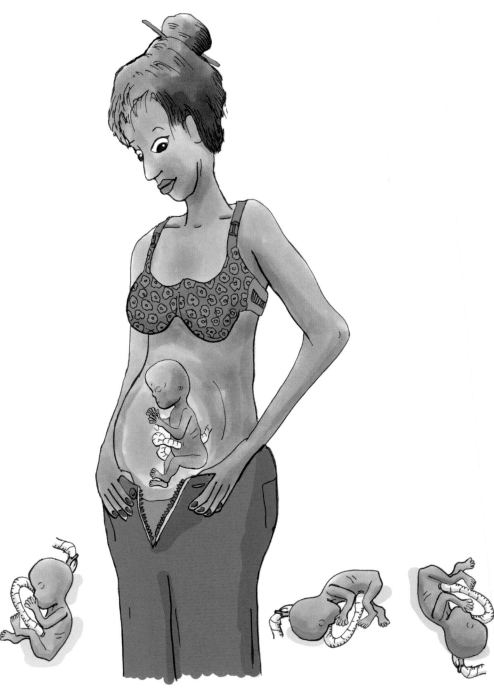

Almost straight away the fertilized egg becomes a bunch of cells, and those cells then form a spine, a brain and a tube called an umbilical cord. Through that cord Bump receives oxygen and nutrients from the mother's body, which are necessary for Bump to continue to grow. Bump floats in a bag of amniotic fluid, which protects against knocks and jolts.

Soon Bump's little heart begins beating, and a face starts to form. Legs and arms grow and so do tiny buds where Bump's teeth will eventually be. Slowly Bump grows hands and feet, fingers and toes and even fingernails and toenails. Eyes and ears take shape and fine hair grows on Bump's body. And while all that is going on, inside parts are growing as well, nerves, muscles, and body organs like a liver, kidneys, stomach, reproductive parts and all the other bits that people need.

After three months Bump is still very tiny but already looks like a baby! There is still heaps of space in the womb to move, so Bump's arms and legs will wave, kick and stretch. Bump may even do somersaults!

As Bump grows bigger, the woman may feel wriggling, fluttering and even kicking in her womb, and her body will grow larger and rounder to make more space.

Did you know that babies hear noises before they are born? It's true! The first sounds Bump hears are the mother's breathing and heartbeat, because those sounds are close by. Later Bump will hear outside sounds as well, such as voices, music, or loud bangs! Sudden noises can make Bump jump! And although there's not much to see inside the womb, as eyes develop, Bump will know when it's light and dark. Lungs are the last organ to develop, and by seven months Bump's lungs will be very close to being ready to breathe.

In the final two months Bump grows quickly and becomes much heavier. Bump spends a lot of time sleeping, and when awake will kick, elbow, wriggle and turn upside down. Bump now takes up lots of space and the mother's tummy is probably feeling big and tight!

The day that Bump is expected to be born is called the due date, and most babies are born close to that date. But not every baby!

Some babies are born early and are very small because they haven't finished growing. Early, or premature babies, usually stay in hospital so they can be looked after while they grow some more. Some babies are born late, and that's called overdue.

Parents make lots of plans and choices during the pregnancy because having a baby changes a lot of things! So let's see how they go about...

PREPARING FOR THE NEW BABY

Knowing how to look after a new baby properly is really important. Some couples go to special classes to learn about birth and how to care for a baby. Some ask advice from their own parents or from friends who already have babies. Others may learn from books.

The couple will decide where the baby will be born, which is usually in a hospital, although sometimes parents choose somewhere different. They'll most likely choose a doctor, or a trained nurse called a midwife, to be there for the birth.

They'll also choose a name or names for the baby, and decide where it will sleep. If one or both parents go to work, they'll need to decide who is caring for the baby. And of course they'll need to buy baby things, like a bassinet or crib, car capsule, pram, baby clothes and all sorts of other things as well!

When everything is ready, the couple will be excitedly waiting for...

THE BIRTH

Often a woman knows when her baby is ready to be born. Perhaps she will get a tummy or back ache, the amniotic fluid bag may break, or she may feel contractions.

Contractions are when the muscles around the womb get tight, and push the baby downwards towards the vagina. Sometimes though, the birth of the baby may happen unexpectedly, and be a bit of a surprise.

Most babies are born through the vagina. The vagina is stretchy, and so the baby moves through, very slowly, until it reaches the outside of the body and is born. That's called a natural birth, and some births take a long time, all day and night, while others don't take long at all. It's hard work for the woman because although the baby fits through the vagina, it's a very tight squeeze.

Usually babies are born head first, but sometimes the feet will come first, and this is called a breech birth. Some babies are even born bottom first!

Not all babies are born through the vagina. A baby may have grown too big, be tangled in the umbilical cord or be in a tricky position. Or it may be sick and needing to be born quickly so that the doctor can care for it.

So sometimes the safest way for the baby to be born is by Caesarian section, or C-section. That's when the doctor makes a cut into the womb and lifts the baby out that way, and it's all okay because the mother doesn't feel any of it. Once the baby is out, the doctor sews up the womb and tummy again.

As soon as a baby is born, it will be checked to make sure it's healthy and takes its first breath and to see if it's a boy or girl.

The umbilical cord is cut and soon the bit of cord still attached to the baby will dry up and drop off, leaving the baby with a belly-button!

Straight after the birth, parents are usually really keen to look at and cuddle their new baby. Then the baby may have a drink, a bath and be wrapped up snug and warm to sleep. Birth is tiring for a baby, too!

Maybe this is a good time for you to ask where and how you were born!

LOOKING AFTER THE NEW BABY

A newborn baby needs liquid meals. The mother may choose to feed the baby by holding it to her breast, where it sucks the milk that her breasts have made. Or she might feed the baby with a specially designed drink called formula, which is sucked from a bottle with a teat at the end.

Besides liquid food, a small baby needs a bath each day, to be changed often, a comfortable place to sleep, regular checkups at the doctor and lots of cuddles. As the baby grows, it will eat solid food, and learn to roll over, sit up and crawl.

It can be a lot of work for parents, who may even be woken at night if the baby can't sleep, but it can also be fascinating watching a baby grow and learn new things.

And some parents have EXTRA work to do because they have...

TWINS OR TRIPLETS

Human mothers usually have one baby at a time, but sometimes two or more babies grow in the womb and are born together. That's called a multiple birth. There's different ways that can happen, and it's something you can ask more about if you're interested.

Two babies are called twins, three are triplets and four are quadruplets, but more than three babies in one birth doesn't happen often at all. Sometimes twins and triplets look the same as each other and sometimes they look completely different. Multiple births can be all boys, all girls or some of each!

I'm sure you've already figured out that looking after two babies is double the work of looking after one!

BOY OR GIRL

Are you wondering how you came to be a girl or a boy? It's simple! Adult males make two types of sperm, X sperm that makes girls and Y sperm that makes boys. So whether you are a girl or boy is because of which sperm, an X or a Y, won the race and fertilized the egg.

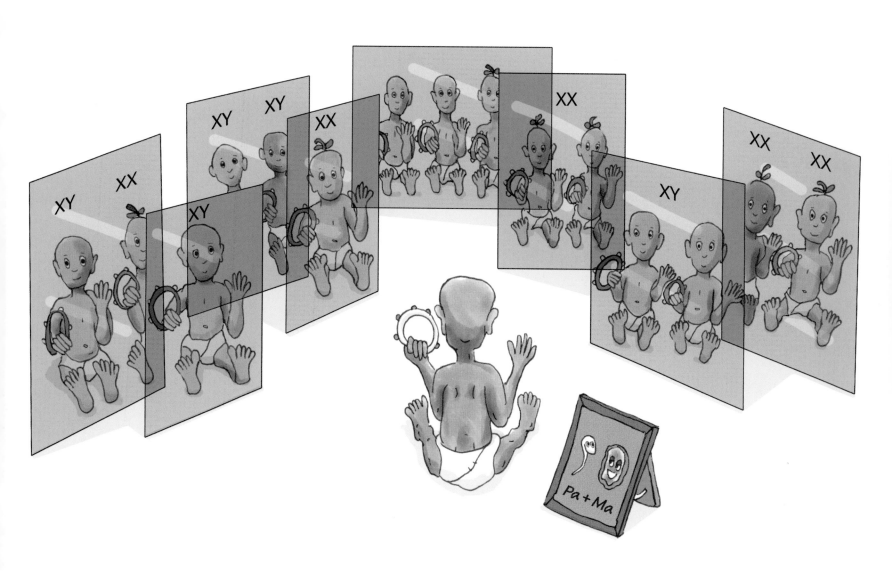

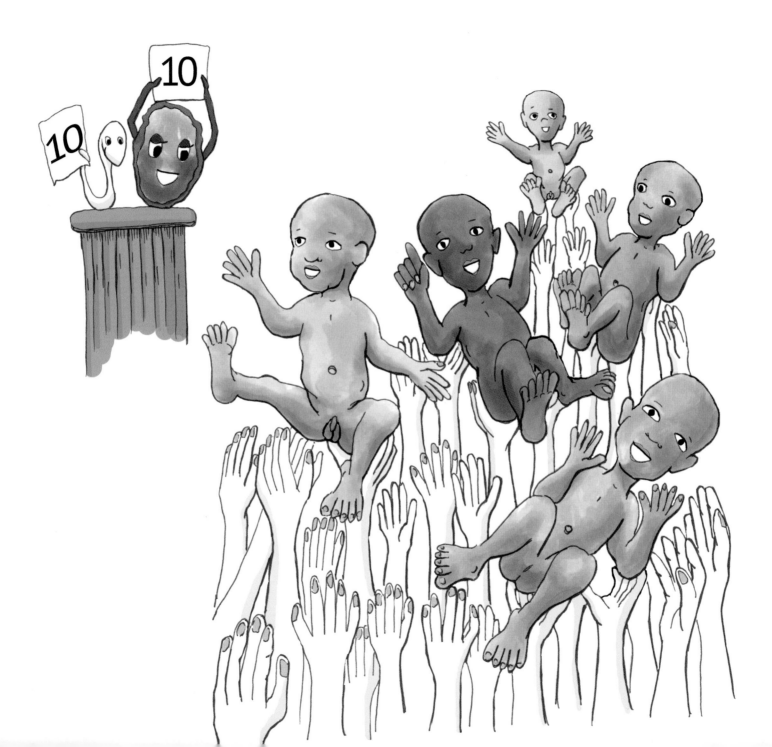

SO THAT'S THAT THEN!

Now you know how you began!

I hope you have enjoyed learning the facts of life! Being curious about bodies and how we are made is natural and healthy, so if you have more questions about how you began it's a good idea to ask your parent, or an adult that you trust very much.

But before I finish, there's one more important thing to tell you.

Every baby is unique... and that means there is no one else in the world who is exactly the same as you!

So...

That means you are very special indeed!

ABOUT THE AUTHOR

Author Gina Dawson is an experienced educator in sexuality and relationship education, having worked for fifteen years presenting programs in schools and to family groups. *So That's How I Began!* was written as a result of requests from parents and caregivers for a balanced book suited to all children, covering modern day families, conception and birth.

Gina's passions are writing children's books that promote awareness about personal and social issues, along with short stories. Her prize winning stories have been published in multiple anthologies and magazines. When not writing the above, Gina assists people write their memoirs and volunteers as a proof reader for charity. Her other interests include, in no particular order, reading, walking, architecture, travelling, exercising her dog, and spending time with family and friends.

So That's How I Began! is her fourth book.

ABOUT THE ILLUSTRATOR

Alex Mankiewicz is an illustrator who was born in NYC, grew up in London and lived in Paris and Japan for years before settling down. She has travelled widely and often to odd corners of the planet, a nomadic life that lends a universality to her art.

For years, Alex worked as a woodblock printmaker in Kyoto. The legacy from that period of an east-west fusion and pared back graphic approach informs her illustration style. Upon returning to England, she studied etching at Central St. Martins, exploration which emphasised the primacy of line.

Commissioned work ranges from editorial to picture books to graphic non-fiction. Individual illustrations have been selected by American Illustration for inclusion in its annuals, and are held in collections in England, France, the US, Japan and Australia.

I dedicate this book to my parents
and the generations that came
before them.

And to my beautiful daughter Rachel who
lives in a world much changed from theirs,
and who never ceases to amaze me.

With love,
GINA

First published in 2018 by New Holland Publishers
London • Sydney • Auckland

131–151 Great Titchfield Street, London WIW 5BB, United Kingdom
1/66 Gibbes Street, Chatswood, NSW 2067, Australia
5/39 Woodside Ave, Northcote, Auckland 0627, New Zealand

newhollandpublishers.com

Copyright © 2018 New Holland Publishers
Copyright © 2018 in text: Gina Dawson
Copyright © 2018 in images: Alex Mankiewicz

All rights reserved. No part of this publication may be reproduced, stored in a retrieval system or transmitted, in any form or by any means, electronic, mechanical, photocopying, recording or otherwise, without the prior written permission of the publishers and copyright holders.

A record of this book is held at the British Library and the National Library of Australia.

ISBN 9781760790233

Group Managing Director: Fiona Schultz
Project Editor: Elise James
Designer: Sara Lindberg
Production Director: James Mills-Hicks
Printer: Toppan Leefung Printing Limited

10 9 8 7 6 5 4 3 2 1

Keep up with New Holland Publishers on Facebook
facebook.com/NewHollandPublishers